PRACTICE
MAKES
PERFECT

A simple approach to *piano technique*

Pauline Hall and Paul Harris

Music Department
OXFORD UNIVERSITY PRESS
Oxford and New York

Oxford University Press, Great Clarendon Street, Oxford OX2 6DP
© Oxford University Press 1994

INTRODUCTION

Learning to play an instrument is a bit like climbing to the top of a mountain: you can't do it in one massive leap — you have to go just a little at a time, taking pains to plan your route very carefully.

When you start learning an instrument, you have to develop all the necessary skills little by little. If you have patience and determination, you'll almost certainly be able to acquire an ability that will give you a lifetime of pleasure.

This book, which will take you from a standard of about Grade 1 to Grade 4, is designed to help you develop your understanding and control of the instrument itself — your *technique* — by a series of progressive stages. Although you will often be asked to work on various aspects of technique separately, don't forget that many are inter-linked. For example, just to play a scale requires correct posture, hand position, correct fingering and finger movement, control of rhythm, and touch!

It's up to you and your teacher how much you practise each day, but if you want to play really well, you should aim to work on technique for about five to ten minutes a day to begin with, and to increase that as you improve.

As practising becomes more of a habit you will be delighted at the results — you'll *want* to practise technique more and more, and you'll certainly realize that:

PRACTICE MAKES PERFECT!

Remember!

If you really want to get the most out of practising technique, always remember that it is not what you practise,

but HOW you practise.

Good practice means:

CONCENTRATE

LISTEN

DO A LITTLE AT A TIME

SET YOURSELF HIGH STANDARDS

STAGE 1

1 Legato playing

To be able to join notes really smoothly (legato playing) is an essential part of your technique.

Make sure that your finger action is firm, but not heavy. Try these exercises in the keys of G, D, and F if you can.

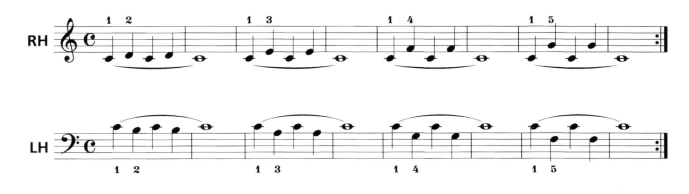

2 Slurs

Slurs *join* notes together. Think of dropping down on the first note and floating up on the second. As you play each bar think '*down-up*'.

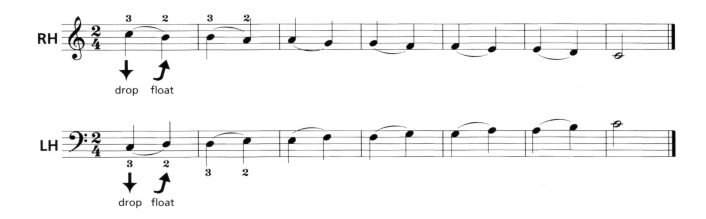

3 Sixths

The interval separating these two notes is a sixth:

Play the sixths at the top of the next page using thumb and 5th finger. Let your arm feel quite relaxed and heavy (as if you were sinking into a comfortable chair) but don't let your finger or wrist collapse. Count four beats for each chord. When you get to the third beat be thinking of sinking down on the next chord.

Have your fingers ready in the '6th' position before you play each chord.

Now repeat the exercise with the left hand an octave lower.

4 Five-finger exercise

Five-finger exercises are to help you strengthen your fingers and develop finger independence. Aim for very even sound and steady and precise rhythm. When you feel you can play the exercise with good control try it at different dynamic levels and include crescendos and diminuendos. Once you can play it well in C major try it in G and F major.

Now repeat the exercise with the left hand an octave lower.

5 Study

6 Posture

How you sit at the piano is extremely important. You should make sure that the piano stool is the right height, so that your arm from elbow to wrist doesn't slope up or down.

Your fingers should be curved and firm, and your arm lightly held so that it supports your hand and doesn't drag it downwards.

If you are using the pedal, your heel should be on the floor.

Sit up straight and *never* slouch.

STAGE 2

1 ## Staccato

Staccato notes must sound crisp and detached. Keep your fingers nicely curved and on their tips. Use your 3rd finger only in this exercise and imagine each key is hot!

2 ## Combining slurs and staccato

As you play each bar think '*down-up-short-short*' or '*short-short-down-up*'.

3 Rotation

This simply means that your arm must feel free to turn. Turn an imaginary door handle — did you notice how your arm rotated? Feel your arm rotating slightly in the following exercises:

4 Accents

If a note is marked with an accent (>) it means that note must be given extra force — in other words, it will be played louder than the other notes in the passage. There are one or two points to remember: if the dynamic marking of the passage is *p* (as in the LH example below), then don't overdo the accented note! It doesn't have to be *fff* — just a firm *f* will do.

Don't allow your fingers, wrist, or arm to become tense when you play accented notes.

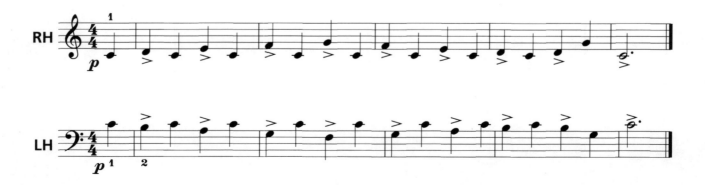

5 Listening game

This will help you to imagine a note in your head and remember it .

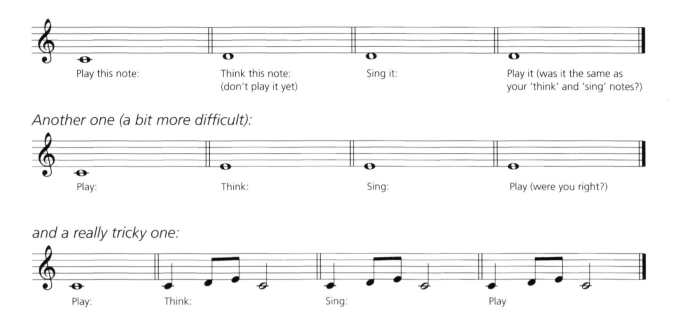

Play this note: Think this note: Sing it: Play it (was it the same as
                    (don't play it yet)   your 'think' and 'sing' notes?)

Another one (a bit more difficult):

Play: Think: Sing: Play (were you right?)

and a really tricky one:

Play: Think: Sing: Play

Invent some more of these to try for yourself.

Know your instrument

To help you learn more about the piano, this book has six projects. Try to find out the answers to these questions, and record them in a notebook. Get your teacher to check your work.

Look out for any pictures in magazines or newspapers to cut out and stick into your notebook: you'll find you can build up an interesting and useful reference book of your own.

Project 1

This project is about the early history of the piano.

1. What were the two important keyboard instruments that Bach, Handel, and the other Baroque composers wrote for?

2. What are the major differences between those instruments and the piano?

3. 'Piano' is only part of the name — what do we call an early piano?

4. Why was the piano called the 'Piano'?

5. Why was Bartolomeo Cristofori important in the history of the piano?

STAGE 3

1 Chords

Play the following exercises slowly and always remember to produce a crisp and detached sound for the staccato notes.

2 Travelling around the keyboard

There are very few pieces where your hands stay in the same place all the time. The next two exercises are to help you develop the ability to move around the piano with confidence and accuracy.

Move your arm as well as your fingers.

3 Wide skips

Practise this so that you can play it accurately without looking at the keyboard!

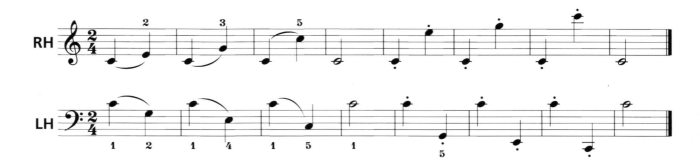

4 Evenness in scale playing — passing the thumb under

One of the most important techniques in playing scale passages really evenly is passing your thumb under smoothly, without any bumps. Practise the following slowly. Speed is not important, but you might like to return to this exercise regularly and try to increase the speed slightly each time.

Always think ahead and have your thumb ready to pass under.

5 Chromatic scales

There are two *golden rules* to remember:

1. 3rd finger on all black notes.
2. 2nd finger only plays where two white keys are next door to each other.

With your right hand play this, going right up the piano:

Now the left hand:

Now try the following:

RH

LH

STAGE 4

1 Mix and match

Try to make each hand take over from the other without any change in sound. The left hand plays notes with stems down, the right hand with stems up.

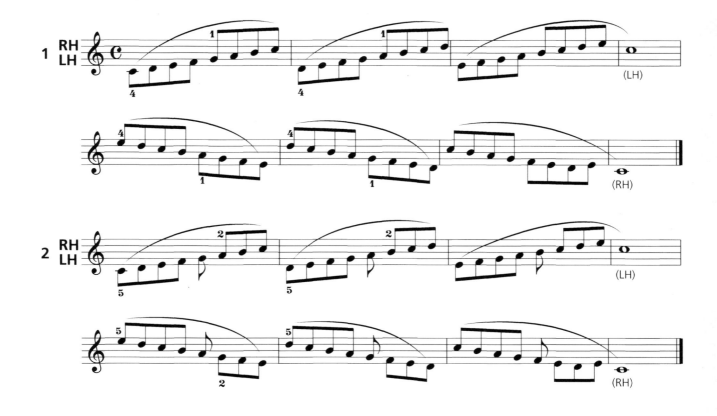

2 Legato pedalling

The sustaining pedal is used for holding notes on — in other words, 'sustaining' them! In the next exercise the pedal goes down with the first chord — hold while you count four — and as soon as you *hear* the next chord, lift the pedal and put it down as quickly as you can.

Make sure that you don't lift your hand from the chord early.

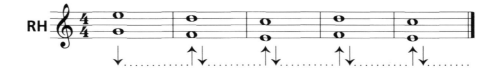

Now try the following, which is the same exercise with an added note in the left hand:

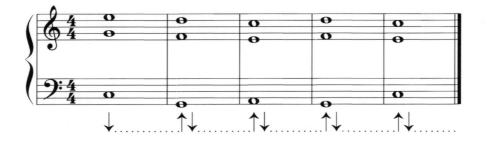

3 Broken chords and scales

This is a good exercise for stretching out and returning your hand to a scale position. Stretch your hand, then move your fingers quickly to the five-finger position.

Play it with each hand separately — left hand an octave below. The fingering is marked, RH above, LH below.

When you can play this exercise with security try it in other keys — G, D, and F.

4 Exercise for the weaker fingers

You will have noticed that your 4th and 5th fingers are less strong than the others; you can strengthen them by practising the next exercise. Make sure that your wrist does not drop when you use your 5th finger. Carry on the pattern as far as you like up the piano. Stop if you feel your hand is getting tired.

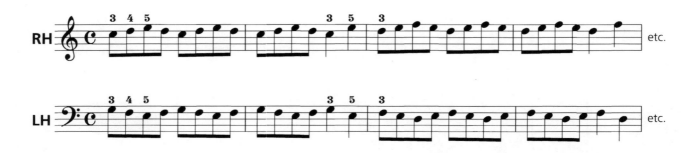

5 Repeated notes

You can of course repeat a note using the same finger, but when the notes are quick, it is really easier to change fingers like this:

Know your instrument

Project 2

This project is about early keyboard music.

1. Which famous composer wrote a set of 48 Preludes and Fugues?

2. Why did he write 48?

3. Another famous eighteenth-century composer wrote a piece called *The Harmonious Blacksmith*. Who was he?

4. Czerny was an important player and teacher (Liszt was among his many famous pupils). What do we now remember him for?

5. Mozart's piano music is among the greatest ever written. Can you discover how many piano concertos he wrote?

STAGE 5

1 More chords

It is a great help in playing chords to recognize their shape. You should therefore train your fingers to find their chord quickly and easily. Prepare your fingers above the keys before you play each chord and make sure all the notes have the same dynamic.

In the next exercise notice how the upper and lower notes stay the same in each bar — only the middle notes move. When you have practised the exercise a few times, add the pedal, up-down on each chord.

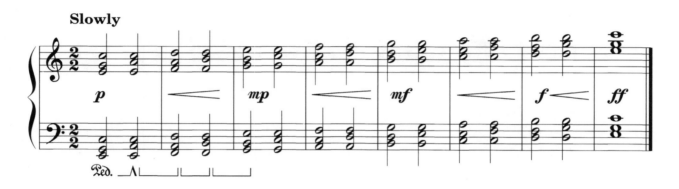

2

Tone control and rotation

Firm fingers are important here. Accents are marked in the first bar, but carry on with the same pattern throughout. Revise the section on rotation (page 6) before working at this exercise.

3 More staccato

In the first study the left hand leads. In the second, it is the right hand.

1 Allegretto

2 Allegretto

Try these exercises in other keys.

4 **Study**

Revise the 'Mix and Match' (page 11) before attempting this study.

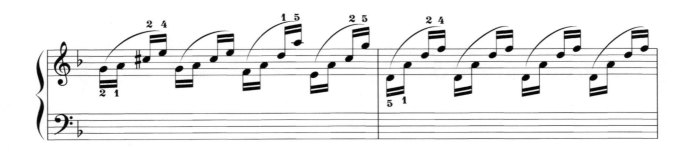

STAGE 6

1 Agility

You will come across many passages that will require really nimble fingers — you won't be able to play them with stodgy or clumsy finger work. Lots of practice on this exercise is a must. Increase the speed as your fingers get to know it.

2 Part playing

In the following exercises each hand has to do two different things. The thumb or 5th finger holds a note while the other fingers play a moving line. This technique is often found in the music of Bach, Handel, and other Baroque composers. Warning: don't release the held notes.

3 Independent hands

The next exercises are to encourage your hands to be independent, by doing different things at the same time — a most important technique to master! First play both exercises as marked, with the RH staccato and the LH legato, then try them the other way around, with the LH staccato and the RH legato.

1 **Andante**

2 **Andante**

4 More finger exercises

Think '*down-up*' as you play the slurred pairs.

18

5 Listening game

This is a test of your inner rhythmic sense. With your teacher, start counting aloud a steady four beats in a bar — 1234, 1234. After two bars continue to count — silently — for another four bars. On the first beat of the fifth bar — clap! Were you both absolutely together?

You could try this in different times, with two or three beats in a bar, or you could vary the speed so long as you keep the beat steady.

Know your instrument

Project 3

This project is to find out something about the instrument itself.

1. How is the sound of the piano produced?

2. How many different types of 'Grand' pianos can you discover?

3. Some pianos have a middle (third) pedal. What does it do?

4. What are the differences between an upright and a grand piano?

5. Bösendorfer is a famous piano-making firm. Its pianos have a rather special feature. Can you discover what this is?

STAGE 7

1 More work on stretching

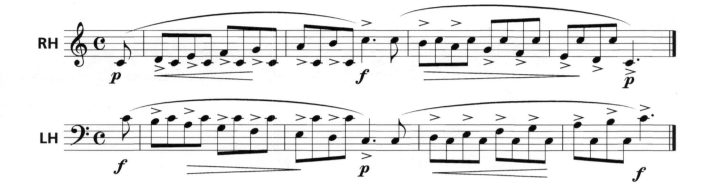

2 Octaves

Don't allow your wrist to become tense in the following exercises. If you can't manage an octave stretch yet (exercise 1), play the sixths (exercise 2) and come back to No. 1 when your hands have grown a bit!

3 Tune with accompaniment in the same hand

There are two things going on at once here, and the right hand is doing them both! The crotchets must be legato and should be louder than the quavers, which are the accompaniment.

4 Fitting notes into a beat

If you have a metronome set it to a very slow pulse. Make sure the first note of each group comes exactly on the beat.

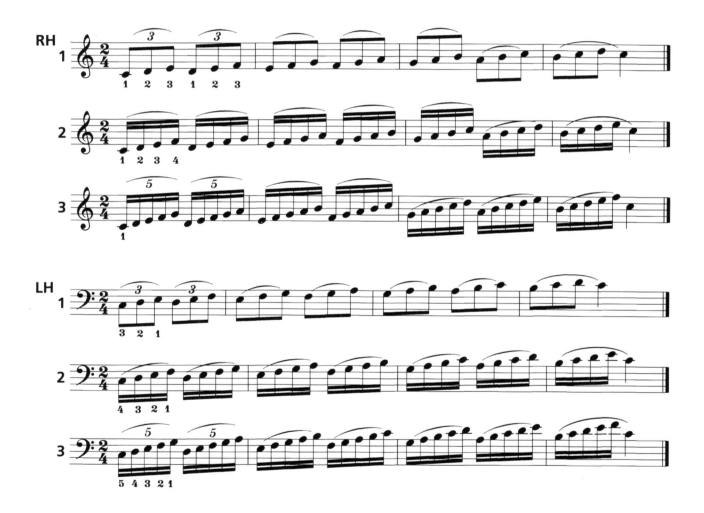

When you can play this accurately with each hand separately try hands together.

5 Listening game

This game will help you to improve your pitch. Play, or get your teacher or a friend to play, any note for four beats. Remain absolutely silent for a period of time (say twenty seconds), then sing the note. Is it the correct one? Is it sharp or flat? Play this again (as often as you like) making the silence longer each time.

STAGE 8

1   Ornaments

An ornament should be ornamental — that is, a decoration. You must not slow down to fit them in.

The Acciaccatura

This actually means a 'crushed' note. Squash it in as close to the main note as you can.

Here are some more acciaccaturas:

Grace notes: play the small notes as quickly as possible before the beat so that the crotchet always falls *on* the beat, but be sure that they have a good sound.

2   Playing scales

Don't forget to practise your scales regularly.
Try them in different rhythms:

a)

b)

c)

Try playing the right hand staccato and left hand legato, and then right hand legato and left hand staccato,

and with expression: $p \lessgtr f \gtrless$ or $f \gtrless p \lessgtr f$

Think up other ways to practise scales yourself.

3 Study

Remember to balance the hands carefully: the left hand is also important in this piece.

23

4 Listening game

Play the following four chords — but not in the printed order. See if your teacher or a friend can work out *your* order. Can you make the dynamic levels really different?

Know your instrument

Project 4

This project is about famous pianists and teachers of the past.

1. Which famous pianist and teacher took holy orders and became an Abbé in later life?

2. Which famous pianist/composer was born in Poland but lived most of his life in France?

3. Another composer who lived in Paris was something of an eccentric. He used to keep monkeys as pets and was tragically crushed to death under a falling bookcase. Who was he?

4. A famous Russian composer wrote four piano concertos as well as much virtuoso music for piano solo. He is considered to be one of the greatest pianists of all time. Who was he?

5. Only one international concert pianist was also a Prime Minister. Who was he, and of which country was he Prime Minister?

STAGE 9

1 Held notes

The following exercises are to help you to develop your finger control and independence. Hold your 2nd and 4th fingers down all through the exercise. Play the other notes, first staccato and, when you can do this, play them legato. You can also practise these exercises away from the piano!

2 Thirds

Your fingers often have to work in pairs: thumb and 3rd; 2nd and 4th; 3rd and 5th. They must play exactly together.

Listen very carefully — the thirds must always be together.

When you can play both these exercises successfully, try them together.

3   Repeated notes

Fingers on their tips here — always aim for a very clear sound.

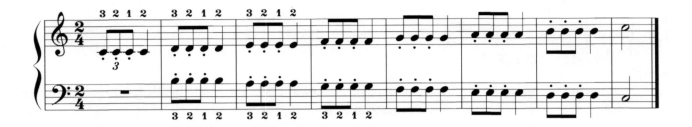

4   Study

5   More work with chords

Practise this exercise using the same fingering pattern throughout.

Notice that your left hand uses $\begin{smallmatrix}1\\5\end{smallmatrix}\ \begin{smallmatrix}2\\4\end{smallmatrix}$ in each chord.

26

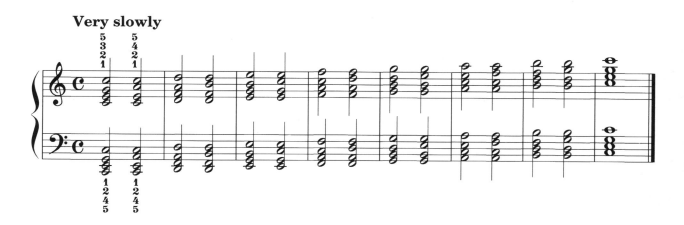

Practise the following with hands separately at first. Change the pedal for each chord.

Very slowly

6 Listening game

A game to improve your sense of pulse.

Counting four beats in a bar, clap on the first beat in bar one; then on the second in bar two, the third in bar three, the fourth in bar four. In bar five clap on the second quaver of the bar, bar six on the fourth quaver, bar seven on the sixth quaver and in bar eight on the eighth quaver. Sounds tricky, but it's well worth the effort! Count the first bar out loud, but after that count in your head and keep your eyes closed.

Try this game with your teacher or a group of friends — the larger the group, the more fun!

Here's the rhythmic shape for reference, but don't actually use it.

STAGE 10

1 ## Finger dexterity

A metronome would be very helpful for the following exercises. Set it at a very slow pulse, two in a bar. Play the exercise in as many keys as you know. You MUST use the correct fingering!

2 ## Octaves and scales

Practise the following exercises hands separately first.

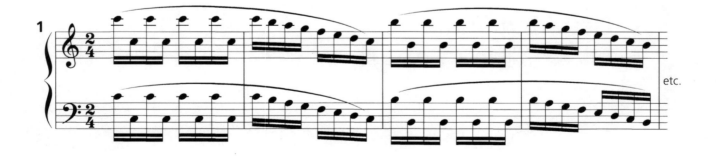

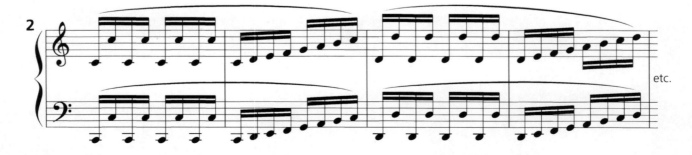

3 Crossing hands

Practise this exercise slowly so that the pulse is not disturbed when you swing your arm across. When you can play it easily, begin to increase the tempo.

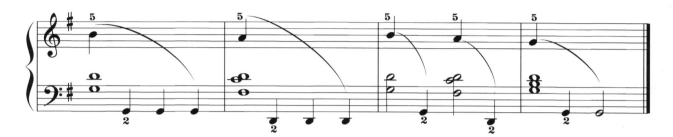

4 Scales in tenths

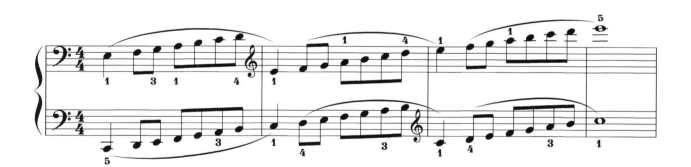

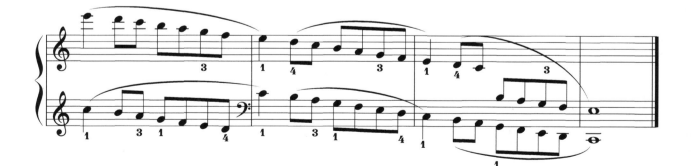

5 More chords

Take your time in the following exercise — hold each chord with the pedal while you are finding the next.

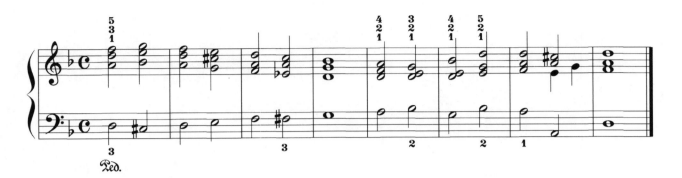

6 Turns

A light arm and neat fingers are needed here. Try these in different keys.

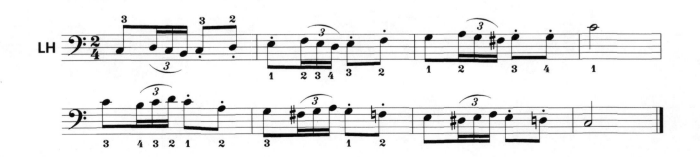

Know your instrument

Project 5

This project is about piano playing today.

1. What is the name of the international piano competition held every three years in England?

2. Who was the founder of the competition (and also a well-known teacher)?

3. Can you discover the names of two concert pianists of today?

4. An American composer wrote pieces for 'prepared piano' — can you discover who this was and how the piano has to be 'prepared'?

5. Can you discover a famous actor and comedian who is also an accomplished pianist?

STAGE 11

1 More chord sequences

Here are various ways you may find chord patterns. Make sure you always use the correct fingering.

First — broken chords:

Secondly — each chord is split in half:

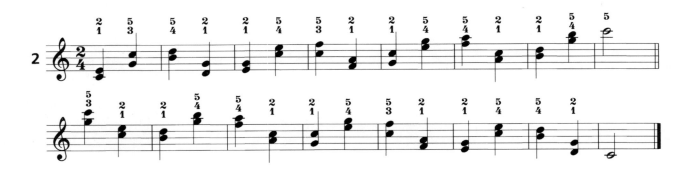

Finally — all four notes of each chord played together. Change the pedal on each new chord. Notice that fingers 1,2, and 5 play in each chord; only fingers 3 and 4 change.

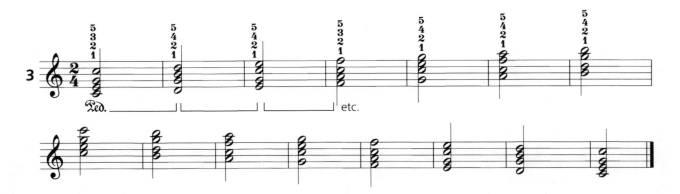

The left hand:

Use the same fingering here:

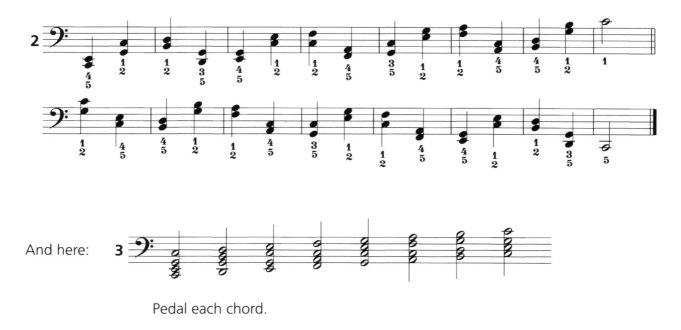

And here: 3

Pedal each chord.

2 6ths and 3rds in sequence

The right-hand fingering is above, the left-hand below (the left hand plays an octave lower). Play this exercise legato and then staccato. Aim for absolute evenness.

(RH)
(LH)

3 Trills

A trill may begin on the note above the main note, or on the note itself. Sometimes it includes a turn at the end. It is important to remember that the pulse must not be affected by the ornament — it must always remain steady.

The first two bars of this study should sound like this:

Listen and count and make sure the last beat of the bar is in time.

Use the 2nd and 3rd fingers for the trills to begin with. When you can play these try the 3rd and 4th fingers.

4 | Two against three

Once you can get the hang of this it becomes quite easy!

Before you play the exercise, tap this rhythm using one hand:

Then using both hands tap the same rhythm:
(T = Together , R = Right, L = Left)

You were actually tapping quavers with your left hand and triplets with your right!

Now try:

Your left hand is tapping the triplets this time.

Now try the following study, slowly at first:

5   Held notes and accompaniment

The crotchets are held and must be played legato. The semiquavers are played lightly as an accompaniment.

6   Changing fingers

You will occasionally have to change fingers on the same note (sometimes known as 'substitution') to achieve a legato. Play the following exercises slowly at first.

STAGE 12

1 Finger exercise

This is a useful exercise for developing more supple fingers. Try it in the keys of D,E,F,G,A, and B major.

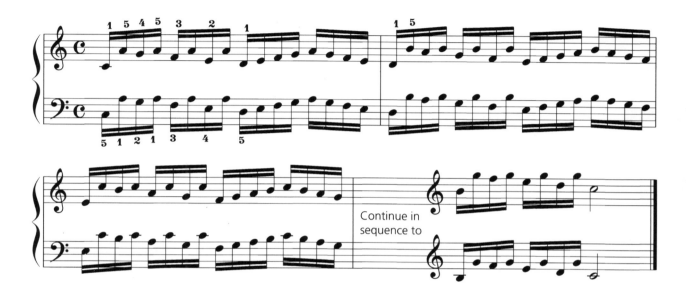

Continue in sequence to

2 Lateral swing

It is important that your arms should feel free to move laterally — that is, sideways. In the next exercise use your 2nd (and 3rd) fingers as a pivot so that your arm can swing easily from side to side.

Change of direction

You should try this in as many different keys as you can, as well as legato and staccato.

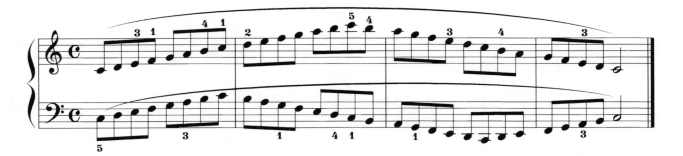

4 **Broken diminished seventh chords**

Each group of semiquavers is played by alternate hands in this study. As soon as one hand has played get it ready for its next group. Pedal each bar and you may like to practise each group as a chord.

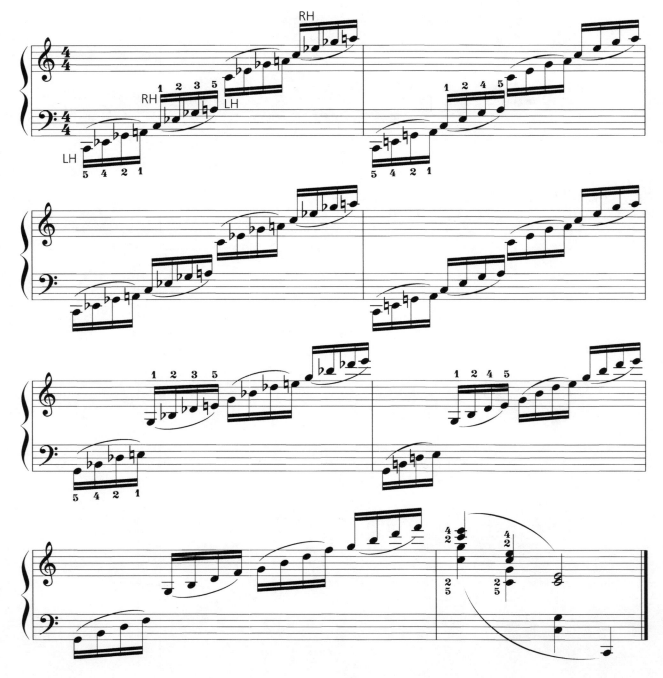

Know your instrument

Project 6

This project is about the piano repertoire.

1. Which important nineteenth-century composer wrote the *Wanderer Fantasy*?

2. Many composers have written variations on a very famous theme by Paganini. Can you discover three?

3. *Für Elise* is probably Beethoven's most famous piano piece, but how many other works for piano by Beethoven can you discover?

4. A piano concerto is written for piano and orchestra. What instruments would you find in a piano quintet? Can you find two composers who wrote piano quintets?

5. Many composers have written pieces especially for children — who wrote a suite of piano pieces called *Children's Corner*?

Typeset by Seton Music Graphics Ltd.
Printed in Great Britain by Halstan & Co. Ltd., Amersham, Bucks.